Jenifer Jobbins, Editor
www.taycreekfestival.ca

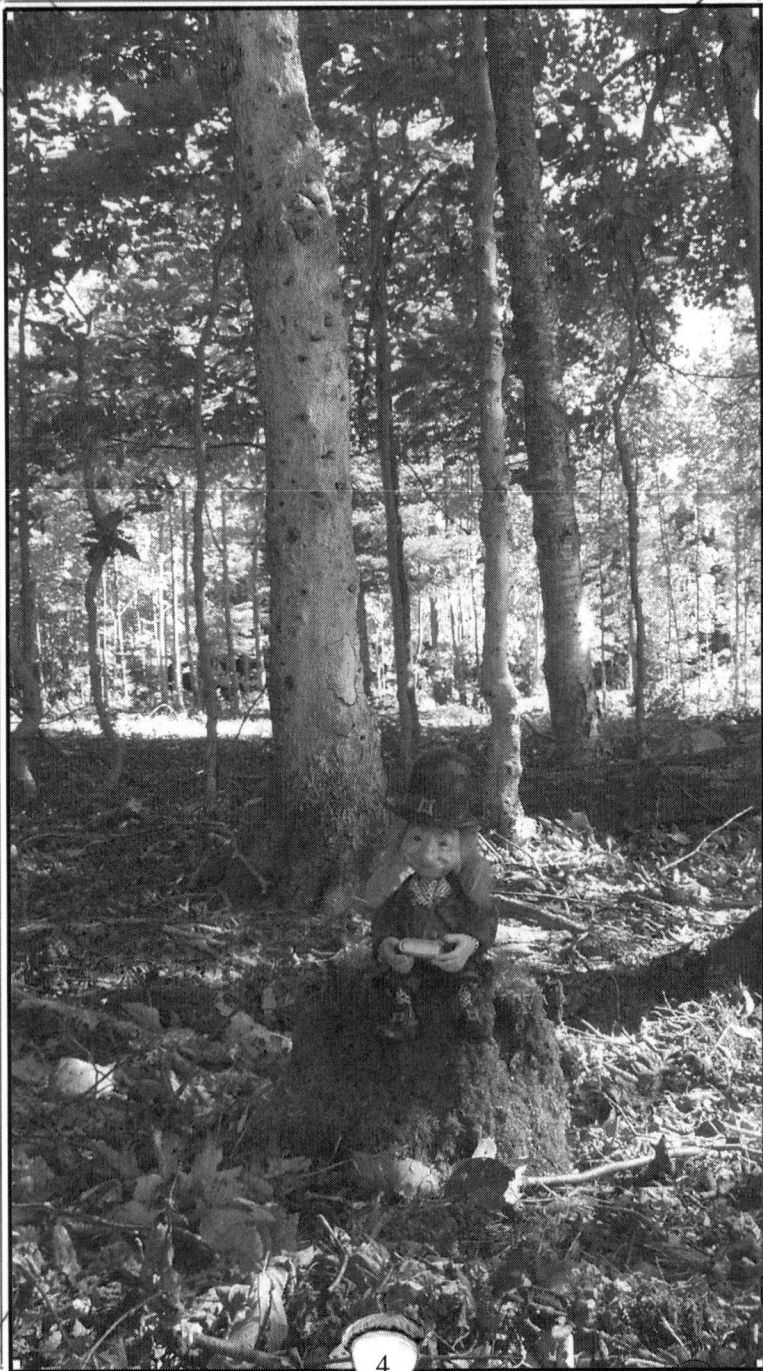

CONTENTS

HOW TO SEE
THE FAERIES

THE COMPLETE CODDLE-POPPER GUIDE

THE LAND OF THE LITTLEPEOPLE.COM

ABOUT THE AUTHORS

Grenville & Debby Woollacott

Ever since we were children, and some people believe we still are, we have both loved Faery tales and often wished that we could see the Faery folk too. But try and try as hard as we could, and it could never be said that we did not try our very best, it just did not happen. As we grew up and the hectic pace of life entangled us, we believed less and less in Faery tales, until they were just a forgotten, distant memory. We became lost in our busy, blinkered World, where there were never enough hours in a day to finish chores, let alone search for Faeries.

We came over from England to Canada in 2005 and fell in love with a beautiful little farm in New Brunswick, and after just a few years we got married. Our wedding was made even more memorable when we were joined for our special ceremony by the Coddle-Poppers and Faery folk that live here. Quite by chance, and after all that time, we realized that we had discovered something most precious, 'The Land of the Little People.' It was then that we decided to name our farm 'Once Upon A Time.'

The next five years we devoted to sharing their antics and learning about all the things that the Coddle-Poppers take responsibility for as 'Mother Nature's Guardians.' Faery tales really do come true!

Since our wedding the farm has been set up to accommodate visitors, who can meander around the many wonderful woodland paths in search of Coddle-Poppers and read their stories while walking along the trails. It is a beautiful place for a picnic with many interesting things to see and do. The wagon ride with the storyteller is an experience not to be missed, as it questions and moves in the grey area between where the Faery tale ends and reality begins. After all, if you can see it, feel it and touch it, how can it be a Faery tale if it can be experienced in such detail? Hmm...

We have to thank our visitors who have inspired and motivated us into writing this book. If you would like to see more about our little farm, please visit our website at

www.**FaeryWood**.com

Yes, it is a real place, and yes, Coddle-Poppers really do exist, as you shall soon discover within the pages of this book.

About Dan Carlson (Music)

Dan is the composer of "Companions," the song which accompanies the audio portion of this book.

In Dan's spare time he enjoys writing and arranging songs. He especially loves barbershop quartet music. He finds it challenging, and rewarding to sing all four parts in harmony and then mix them together to create his own quartet. What better way to match voices in four-part harmony. He also adds his voice and composes songs using the computer to create the instruments and background music. You can hear more of his work at: www.weefolk.com/danmusic/dans_music.htm

Dan's day job is the management of Wee Folk Creations, which he and his wife, Maureen, began in the late 1970's. Their first efforts centered around selling the original clay characters that Maureen created from polymer clay. Eventually they began producing push molds, books, videos and classes, all of which were designed to make it easier for people to create their own clay characters. Maureen has developed several licensed lines of characters, including Sister Folk, Friar Folk and Pippsywoggins: Little Friends from the Edge of Imagination. And, like Grenville, Maureen is a fantasy storyteller too. You can read all thirty-six Pippsywoggin stories at http://www.weefolk.com/pips.htm#stories

The Carlsons live in Minnesota where they can often be found watching the ever-changing waters of Sand Creek, which flows just steps away from their back door.

About Jesse Giffin (Illustrator)

Jesse Giffin is an emerging Graphic Designer & Illustrator, and recent graduate of the New Brunswick College of Craft & Design, in Fredericton, NB. Though originally from Winnipeg, Jesse has been living in the Maritimes since 2005.

Inspired by both the natural and technological worlds, Jesse creates in a large variety of mediums and styles, from acrylic painting to digital illustration. In 2014 Jesse received the ArtsNB Media Arts Scholarship in recognition of his work.

For contact information and to see more of his work, please visit:

W W W . J G A R T D E S I G N . C O M

ABOUT THIS STORYBOOK

Life will never be the same again once you expand the imagination to a new level of thinking. It will reveal a whole new dimension that exists right here in front of our very eyes without us even realising. How exciting is that?

We use these storybooks to teach a great moral message and apply the imagination to the possibility of a whopping great big, **'What if …?'**

With this series of Coddle-Popper storybooks you will learn that anything really **is** possible and that Faery tales are as much for grown-ups as for children.

You are never too old for Faery tales. Size really does **not** matter and what each and every one of us can do in order to make life **purposeful**.

The discovery of the Coddle-Poppers and how to see them is just an added bonus that makes life simply magical. Visitors to our farm inspired us to write these books as they were unable to see the line where the fairy tale ends and reality begins. Especially when you can experience it in such amazing detail!

We promise that if you invest in yourself just long enough to read the first chapter, you will smile enough to keep reading, and if you don't we offer a thirty-day no-quibble guarantee that if we don't make you smile you can have your money back. Is that fair?

Turn the pages and you will discover all about the magical world of the 'North American Coddle-Popper' and we shall also pull the plug on the biggest secret ever! That is, how your imagination re-engages with the magic in life.

ACKNOWLEDGEMENTS

We would like to take this opportunity to thank the most gracious Coddle-Popper King and Queen at 'Once Upon A Time' for granting us access to their Kingdom of 'The Land of the Little People' in order that we may share their incredible stories.

We would also like to show our appreciation to 'The Counsel of Coddle-Popper Elders,' for without their kind co-operation we would never have been allowed to spend the last five years researching and having access to share their diverse and amazing daily routines.

We would also like to extend our gratitude to each and every Coddle-Popper that opened not just their doors, but their hearts as well, and allowed us to take a peek inside their homes, their World, and their lives.

We dedicate this book to you all, and hope that one day soon all Coddle-Poppers will once again be able to walk freely through the woods as you do, without fear of being captured just for being a little different from the likes of the rest of us. Thank you.

HOW TO SEE
THE FAERIES
THE COMPLETE CODDLE-POPPER GUIDE

PART 1

THE SITUATION

The number of times that we are asked where the Coddle-Poppers live is nobody's business. Do we see them is another question that's as regular as a high fibre diet. How do we know that they are there is also quite popular, and even the unthinkable … do they really exist? Holy rolling-thunder, sprinkles and Faery dust, as if we'd make something up like that!

We took a list of the most commonly asked questions to the Counsel of Coddle-Popper Elders at the 'Faery Wood' Chapter of Healing Owl in order that they might be made aware of the folly of human disbelief. We hope the Coddle-Poppers might come up with a plan as to how we can reveal the answers to all of these questions, concerns and perhaps even more.

After all, it is perfectly okay to question these things, but it really is quite another when folk fail to believe it! So the onus for proof must be for each individual to be able to see it for themselves, with their own eyes or the eyes of a close relative.

That being said, once shown, if that person still won't believe their own eyes, well that is another problem for another day, as that person suffers from an acute shortage of magic in their life and no amount of Faery dust in the world, or even in their eye is ever going to change it for them until they are ready to change it for themselves, and no Coddle-Popper or Faery will try to convince them otherwise.

The difficulty facing The Counsel of Coddle-Popper Elders is that humans live in the 'Middle World' and Coddle-Poppers and Faery folk live in the 'Lower World,' or the 'Other World' as they like to call it, and the confusion is caused because of the fact that Coddle-Poppers and Faeries are regularly seen out and around in our world as they go about their daily chores.

THE SOLUTION

After much deliberation, copious amounts of Coddle-berry wine and enough fungal-crunch bark clippings to bring a hippo to its knees, an idea had finally occurred! It turned out to be quite a simple solution really, especially by Coddle-Popper standards. Yes sir, not that their standards are very high anyway because the tallest Coddle-Poppers are only six inches tall and what use is a standard if it is unreachable?

It can be safely established that Coddle-Popper standards are less than six inches.

Everybody knows that each and every human child starts off with the usual, standard issue of one imaginary friend; unfortunately, as the child gets older the discomfort created by peers and grown-ups causes the imaginary friend to be pooh-poohed to the back of the child's mind. A very sad human dis-ease indeed.

If the Coddle-Popper could just take human grown-ups back to the magical, inquisitive mind of childhood, all could be revealed because your imaginary friend is still there waiting for you, like the most loyalest of little puppy dogs, in the vain hope that 'just maybe' you

might want to spend some time together again. Oh how wonderful that would be! The World would certainly begin to change for the better.

All that the Coddle-Poppers needed was some type of time machine, but the problem faced by the Counsel of Coddle-Popper Elders was that Coddle-Poppers have no concept of time, and if there is no time, what use would a time machine be as the only time there is, is **now**? This called for more Coddle-berry wine and Fungal-Crunch bark clippings.

Eventually, the Counsel of Coddle-Popper Elders finally decided that the use of a time machine would be impractical, so each and every one of them has volunteered their services to take you there themselves, just to show you. So buckle up and fasten your seat belts, we're going on a journey with the Coddle-Poppers down to the wild and wonderful world of Faery, in order to meet up with either a Faery, a Guardian Spirit or your favourite Coddle-Popper. Woo-hoo! How exciting, it feels like Christmas, but of course that could also be the Coddle-Berry wine effect!!

In case you are wondering what a Guardian Spirit might be, some of the more enlightened humans receive great comfort from a tree,

plant or the energy source of where you find peace in nature, and to see the spirit of such a valued companion would be quite an extraordinary experience in itself!

We heartily recommend that everyone should hug a tree, or spend some time in nature and talk away their troubles at least just once. Trees are awesome listeners and if you are able to listen too, trees are very therapeutic and will exchange your sad energy for healing energy, and the results will have you hooked and going back again and again. Yes sir.

In order to be respectful, we use the old term of 'Faery' with an 'e,' rather than 'Fairy' with an 'i,' because Faery includes all of the Faery folk such as Coddle-Poppers, Pixies, Gnomes, Leprechauns, Elves and not just the Fairies as we know them at 'Healing Owl' and 'Faery Wood.'

As strange as this may seem, Faery also includes things that go bump in the night - and even the Angels from the higher realms too, and that is why Archangel Michael, who is protector of all, will accompany us in order to be assured of protection while we are led on our journey by a merry band of overly enthusiastic and slightly pickled Coddle-Poppers.

The Lower World, or 'Other World' as Coddle-Poppers call it, often have 'shamans' come to visit. Shamans journey through a tunnel or portal into the earth. A shaman is a person who can enter a meditation-type trance and journey to other dimensions and realities in order to communicate with its inhabitants and gain spiritual knowledge.

This means that the Faeries are used to seeing humans around, which means that it's safe for us to visit too.

For today's adventure we shall follow in the shamans' footsteps and do the same. There are many ways to do this and some of you may already have your own method. But this is the way that we do it, which you might still find useful even as a seasoned meditator.

We imagine ourselves going through the magical doors of the Coddle-Poppers' Sacred Stump located here at Faery Wood and have included it on the cover of this book and CD to make it easier for you to visualise. This is the portal that we use as our gateway to the 'Other World.'

The 'Other World' where we're going might

seem rather earthy at first, and is uncannily similar to our 'Middle World' with its rivers, woods and countryside. The beings inhabiting the 'Lower World' are the Spirits of animals, trees, plants and rocks, as well as human-like Spirits that are connected with the legends, folk-lore and myths of the earth.

You will also notice that we make reference to Creator; there are many names for your higher powers, depending on your own religious beliefs.

You might refer to your own **higher power** as God, Jesus, Buddha, Allah, or the wife, … or whomever else that your own denomination refers. You will also find that sometimes we also refer to Creator as Source or Spirit too.

There is no wrong or one way to refer to Spirit, as we are all source beings created from the same source energy, our only difference is that we each have our own unique terminology for our own particular higher power, but what is most important is your love and intention, so from here forward, whenever we say Spirit or Creator, to you it will mean the name that you use for your own higher power.

PREPARATION FOR MEDITATION

Preparation is everything. Failing to plan is like planning to fail, so take your time with these simple exercises. You may not be aware of the subtle changes that your body makes, but the Faery-folk definitely will, and these changes will help them communicate better with you - which is the whole point of this journey, isn't it?

Meditation helps us to communicate more easily with the Coddle-Poppers and Faery-folk. It also makes our lives more enjoyable and balanced.

The Faeries get a kick out of doing all of these simple mental exercises in concentration with us because they are the first ones to be distracted ordinarily. Why else do you think Faeries carry shiny wands!! These exercises will help you find the still silent place within.

Going one step further, if you can get into a habit and meditate on a daily basis, you will find that your psychic and intuitive abilities will gradually unfold like the daisies in the early morning dew.

Of course, you can still learn to do these abilities, even if you don't meditate, but it takes soooo much longer and it is much, much harder to be any good at it.

DE-CLUTTERIZATION

That's a Coddle-Popper word which means 'removal of busy-ness'. Oh Lordy! Busy-ness is also another Coddle-Popper word which means 'having too many distractions to be fully engaged in the present moment,' which in the Faery World is jokingly referred to as 'finding something shiny.'

It's really important that we put our busy-ness to one side so that we can tap into the love and healing from the World of Faeries, because there is so much of it that they want to share with us.

Too many people try to meditate while their minds are bogged down in emails, 'to-do' lists, Facebook, or still stuck on whoever did whatever to them during the day.

By not letting go of all this junk that you are holding on to, there is less room to receive all the gifts that are being given because your mind is still taken up by busy-ness and it is your heart, rather than your hands, that is holding on to the clutter.

So take some deep breaths because we're going to do a couple of things to empty your hands

and heart of busy-ness for a short while, so as to allow extra room for gifts from the Faeries.

We're going to do this meditation/journey to the 'Other World' with all of our senses fully engaged.

We shall move through the Lower World smelling the fragrances, seeing the beauty, feeling the textures and listening to the amazing sounds.

Take more deep breaths because we want to smooth out our energy. Breathing helps you center. It's a way to help you come to a place of balance. So take time to settle into your chair, or wherever you're listening from, and settle into yourself.

Before we open our senses, I'm going to say some words first, and I want you to notice how these words shift your vibration, because essentially what we're doing with this meditation/journey is shifting our vibration to a higher, more positive frequency. Everything in life is vibration.

We shall shift from the dense state of consciousness of our Material World, into a more spiritual state of consciousness that is the Faery World.

Each of these words has meaning and will shift your vibration towards a place of beauty.

Feel what happens on a cellular level in your body when you hear these words:

Happiness ... peace ... amazement ... harmony ... joyousness ... exquisite ... inspiration ... beautiful ... truth ... passion ... smiley-face ... love ... chuckle-bunny ... gratitude ... gorgeous ... radiance ... laughter ... wonderment ... gloriousness ... snuggles.

Notice how your energy shifted as you took in the vibration of those words.

Now think of a favourite person or pet. It could be a puppy. It might be a tree or a baby. Maybe it's your favourite Aunt Flossy! Think about those that make you smile, and feel your own inner smile growing inside.

Imagine touching your favourite fabric. It may have been your blanky when you were younger, or stroking your pet if that's what makes you feel happy. It could be the sensation of bare feet in the warm sand of a beach, or the silkiness of a material that you wear. Really let yourself feel it and allow it to make you smile.

Imagine hearing the beautiful sounds of birds singing or hearing the sound of laughter. It might even be listening to the rain that makes you feel calm. What sounds bring you joy or makes you smile?

Now engage your sense of smell. Smell the beautiful fragrances that you love in nature. I love the smell of freshly mown grass. It could be a favourite flower. Really take it in. Take a chomp of your favourite food or a sip of one of your favourite drinks. Swallow it. Feel it going down. Mmm, mmm, feels good doesn't it?

Notice now that you're feeling different. More alive, present and aware now that you've opened your senses more. As you engage your imagination, you begin to leave your busy-ness behind you.

Now that you're feeling more present after experiencing your favourite tastes, textures, sounds and smells, this breathing exercise will help you focus on focusing.

Make sure that you sit upright for this one. Rest your feet on the floor and relax your shoulders. Close your eyes. Concentrate on your breath. Be aware of it coming in, and going out.

Notice how your body moves as you breathe.

Keep doing the deep breaths.

Just like the sea where the waves roll in and out. Notice your breath naturally changes as you keep doing this, becoming deeper the more relaxed you become.

You don't really need to do anything more to make this happen because it just happens. Let your breath move in its own time and at its own pace.

GROUNDING & CENTERING

By connecting with Mother Earth, you allow her to clean and restore your energy by means of an exchange. When you give Mother Earth the gift of your energies, you will receive the gift of her healing energy in return. Result right?

You see, really, there is no such thing as good or bad energy. Energy just is! It is our own human thinking that makes it so. There's also no need to feel bad about giving Mother Earth all of your negative energy either, as all she has is love in return. As we grow spiritually we shall realize this and all there will be is unconditional love. But for now, we're flushing the human frailties of negative energy and replacing it with the good stuff!

Learning awareness of and developing the strength and flexibility of your energy field can be lots of fun and, with practice, grounding will get easier and quicker.

According to the Coddle-Popper, sacred space is the space between the 'exhale' and the 'inhale,' and to be in balance is to have Heaven (spiritual realm) and Earth (physical realm) in harmony.

This means being balanced in your own being and looking out at the world from the perspective of your higher power; which might take a bit of practice if this is not your natural way of being.

How would I know if I'm centered? You might ask! Well, if you're not centered in yourself, then instead of minding your own knitting, you're usually up to something, or meddling in some other person's business!

To center yourself, sit with your feet flat on the floor and relax your shoulders; we're going to take your chakras for a whirl. Chakras are your power center and part of your energy body. They're like spinning energy vortexes that radiate from your body.

Imagine that the bottom of your feet are growing roots, and that they are planting themselves deeper and deeper into the ground and spreading wider and wider, the same way that a tree spreads its roots.

Now, I want you to pretend that you're able to breathe from your roots and inhale your breath up your legs, through your root chakra, into your body. The root chakra is located at the tip of your tailbone and establishes the deepest

connections with our physical body, our environment and with Mother Earth. It is the root of our being.

Allow your breath to come through your root chakra into your pelvis. Located at the bottom of your pelvis is your sacral chakra. The sacral chakra is for experiencing our lives through feelings and sensations.

Allow your breath to continue on past your belly button to your solar-plexus chakra. The solar plexus chakra is your power center, your core self. This is for your personal power. It is the center of your self-esteem, your willpower and your warmth and personality.

When you breathe back out, follow your breath back through the solar-plexus chakra, sacral chakra, and root chakra, down your legs and back into the roots.

When you breathe back in through the roots again, follow the same path back up through your chakras. Just above the solar plexus is the heart chakra. The heart chakra is your love and healing center.

Allow your breath to continue through your healing center to the bottom of your neck, where the throat chakra is located. The throat chakra is for communication. The throat chakra allows you to seek knowledge that is true and allows you to speak your truth.

Let your breath continue to your brow chakra, located just above your eyes. The brow chakra is also referred to as your third eye. The gift of the brow chakra is seeing both inner and outer worlds; this gives us clear thought and self-reflection.

As you breathe back out, allow your breath to return through the brow chakra, throat chakra, heart chakra, solar plexus chakra, sacral chakra, root chakra, down your legs all the way back down to your roots.

Breathe back in again through the roots, up your legs, through your root chakra, sacral chakra, solar plexus chakra, heart chakra, throat chakra, brow chakra and allow your breath to go all the way to the top of your head. This is your crown chakra. The crown chakra connects us with the universe and the divine source that created us. This gives us a sense of knowing and a feeling of unity.

Picture now a bright white light of energy coming from Creator, down through the top of your head, through the crown chakra, blowing out the cobwebs from our body as it sends our energy vortexes whirling, blowing out any blockages as it cleanses the energy with every breath in and out, as it passes up and down through all our chakras, from the top of your head to the tips of your roots.

Rinse and repeat this process until you experience freshness and vitality. Note how lovely it feels to be so refreshed. This, my friends, is centering and leaves you firing on all cylinders and almost ready to go on a journey with the Coddle-Poppers!

When we are centered, we know how we really feel about things, and we have clarity about what is, or is not, appropriate for us.

It is worth mentioning here. that even though you now feel like a million dollars, occasionally in life we don't like how we feel, and it's easy to be tempted to deny our feelings and become un-centered.

TOP TIP:

It's far better in the long run to acknowledge your feelings, no matter how painful, and face the situation or issue head on.

There's always a Coddle-Popper ready to help

us with this, if we ask. If this ever happens to you, then try this exercise.

CONNECTION

We shall cover this in more detail as we do the journey, but here are a few fundamentals to take on board before we start. Connection can best be described as establishing a rapport with our still quiet voice, and Creator. Connection allows us to intuitively access the World of Faery and other sources of wisdom.

We begin by thanking Spirit for the help that they have given in the past, and ask for their guidance for the greater good of all involved in what we are doing now and also for our personal intentions and ego to step aside.

Keep your prayer simple; it doesn't need to be complicated. A few brief words straight from your heart are far better than any elaborate string of memorized words that might sound good, but don't really have any feeling.

Focus on the feeling of connection using gratitude and open your heart to allow the love and wisdom to come to you. Connection to our higher power is usually done through our mind, but the importance of connecting with our heart is sometimes overlooked, especially when we are looking for compassion and wisdom.

So, for a final recap before we start our journey with the Coddle-Poppers:

'Meditation' quiets the mind in order for us to hear the still, quiet voice. This also enables us to listen to what messages the Faeries and Spirit Guides might wish to share with us.

'De-clutterization' gets rid of the distractions of the day and raises our vibration.

'Grounding' keeps us down to earth, even though Coddle-Poppers and Faeries can have us up in the air about matters and lead us on a merry dance.

Being **'Centered'** helps us discern what might be right for us when we hear it.

Being **'Connected'** opens our minds and our hearts to the wisdom given to us by Spirit Guides and Faeries.

When we are all of the above, we are fully immersed in the wholeness of being and in a magical place where miracles usually happen.

WHAT TO EXPECT

Here's a brief heads-up of what's going to happen! When we get down to the Lower World, we'll first acclimatize to our surroundings. The Counsel of Coddle-Popper Elders will ensure that we are not disturbed, to give us time to be comfortable. We shall walk along the riverbank to the Coddle-Popper village of Buttercup Meadow in the Wood.

The Coddle-Poppers have promised to remain silent, so as not to frighten off some of our less experienced meditation/journeyers, and they will line up along the path and will not approach you. The onus will be on you to approach them, as and when you get more comfortable with the experience.

Friendly Fairies will also be there to lead the way, after the excitement has subsided. You will hear the Fairies floating all about and just maybe … if you're lucky enough, a Fairy might pick up on your vibration and trust you enough to let you to be near them. Oh my, what an honour that would be!

If you are that lucky you will definitely know when this happens, as they will gently let you

know and you will know that they know that you know even though nothing gets said. Yes sir, how cool and Fairy-like is that!

The Coddle-Popper King and Queen have assured us safe passage through to a clearing on the far side of the singing trees, where we shall meet our favourite Coddle-Popper, Faery or Guardian Spirit. Whichever one, it is of your choice.

If you feel confident enough to invite whomever it is that you will be meeting to come closer, then it is heartily recommend to please do so.

They will surely answer your question, or perform a healing on your behalf. All that you need to do is just state your question or intention to them and then open up all your senses.

Take note whether you see an image, hear a message, feel a knowing or notice any other feelings that might arise in your body. The hairs on my arm stand on end as a confirmation for me. It may even be a smell that gives you a memory link.

If you are not yet comfortable to invite the Coddle-Popper, Faery or Guardian Spirit closer, that's okay too and for your own peace of mind it may be best not to do so.

Just soak in the atmosphere and maybe on your next meditation/journey, try it then. It is more important that you enjoy your experience at your own pace, rather than force yourself to do something that you are not yet comfortable with, or ready to embrace.

That is the beauty of this book/audio, as you can have this wonderful experience as many times as you wish, so take as much time as you need and make sure to have fun with the experience.

If for this journey you are asking for healing, allow yourself to soak in the loving energies that your Coddle-Popper, Faery or Guardian Spirit shares with you and feel them transform your pain or illness.

Another good tip is **NOT** to push the pace of this journey. Relax into it and keep breathing deeply. All through the journey we will guide you all the way while we drum.

Use your senses, the smells, the beauty, the sounds, touch things, be aware of your feel-

ings, the emotions that come from them and remember to ask lots and lots of questions and note what comes from the still quiet voice within.

At the point where it is time to ask your Guardian Spirit or favourite Coddle-Popper your question or receive a healing, we shall just drum and not speak until it is time to return.

When we do return, we shall give you notice, then guide you back. Remember, don't think too hard, relax, and have fun; you cannot do this wrong, and the only person you need to satisfy is **YOU**.

JOURNALING

O ne of the greatest gifts that you can give yourself is a record of all your magical experiences. It reveals to you your spiritual growth as a person. If you read it a couple of times in a year, I shall eat my hat if you don't find an amazing change in the way that you perceive things, because perception is part of the transformational process.

Journaling is one of the easiest and most powerful ways to accelerate your personal development. By getting your thoughts out of your head and putting them down on paper, you gain insights you'd otherwise never get to see.

Have you noticed how it is easier to solve someone else's problems rather than your own? That is because you are able to look at it from a different perspective.

We can't solve our own problems with the same thinking that we used when we created them. Albert Einstein proved that.

We need to rise above the issue to the next level and look down on it with a bird's eye perspective.

By writing our experiences down and letting

go, when we come back to them, we feel our thoughts in a whole new enlightened perspective.

Some problems are very tricky to solve, especially if you're stuck in the same mind-set that created it. If you've written it down, stepped back a bit and then read it from a third-person perspective, or as though the problem belongs to a friend, the solution reveals itself to you.

Sometimes the answer is so obvious, and right in front of your nose, that you're shocked that you hadn't seen it sooner!

It's also awesome to go back and re-read your meditation journal entries from a while ago and see how much progress you've made.

When life doesn't seem to be as rosy as you'd like, as it sometimes does, go back and read something you wrote a long time ago - it will totally blow your mind and change your perspective.

This helps you in the present moment too by reminding you that you are in fact growing and changing, even though you might feel like

you're standing still. It will show you just how far you have come!

We have left some pages free at the back of this book so that you can remember forever your very first 'Journey with the Coddle-Poppers,' and it will always be here for reference whenever you need it.

Remember to include your question as well as the answers received.

ENERGY EXCHANGE

The Universe rolls with the 'Law of Reciprocation.' You need to give in order to receive.

Maybe as a thank you, leave a piece of chocolate on a rock for the Faeries. Faeries love chocolate, especially Coddle-Poppers! Better still, pay the deed forward with an act of kindness to another.

The more you give, the more you get. And when you see what your giving means to someone, you receive all over again. Now that's a Coddle-Popper win-win double doozie, if ever there was one. Yes sir.

A brilliant idea would be to bring some chocolate with you when we go on our journey to the Lower World. I feel sure that you'll get the opportunity to share it with them.

OM

There is a spiritual essence called source energy. This source energy connects everyone, and everything, with the heart of Creator. The sacred word that the trees sing is 'Om.'

We can experience this essence as both sound and light. Singing the 'Om' is a way to experience the light and sound of Creator.

The singing trees affectionately call the 'Om' their love song to Creator.

Life is a school for each individual, where he or she learns to live in creative harmony with all aspects of life including nature.

Anyone can work with the 'Om' regardless of age, background or religion.

ATTITUDE OF GRATITUDE

Coddle-Poppers keep a magical coin in their pocket with 'One Special Wish' just waiting to be given to a deserving person. Every time that they feel it in their pocket, they say a big thank you for all the special people in their life, and all the wonderful things that they have.

Don't worry if you don't have a magical coin with 'One Special Wish.' Humans can still practice this feeling by using any attractive looking pebble, or better still, a crystal. Begin with a big thank you for all the special people in your life, and all the wonderful things that you have and take it from there.

The Coddle-Poppers call it an 'Attitude of Gratitude.' Yes sir, it is a very good attitude to have and it never hurts to give the coin, or pebble, a gentle rub once in a while to encourage the magic. No sir; it certainly does not hurt one little bit.

This is the simplicity of how the 'Attitude of Gratitude' works ... By being a kind person, you must have seen a reaction of gratitude from a loved one when you did something special for them. When you saw just how happy it made

them, you then wanted to do even more for that person, didn't you?

It is a wonderful feeling. One of the best feelings in the World and it doesn't cost a single thing, but is worth more than money can buy. Yes Sir, it doesn't get better than that, does it? Well, only if it came with a piece of chocolate cake, with a squirt of cream on top … and maybe perhaps some ice cream too.

You can find out more about the 'Attitude of Gratitude' in our next storybook titled, **'The Tree of Wishes.'** Yet another life changing experience, courtesy of the Coddle-Poppers.

We now recommend for you to put down this book, or pause the recording here, so as to allow you enough time to do these exercises in your own time, and at your own pace. But please bear in mind, that when we commence the journey with the Coddle-Poppers in the next part, it will be our assumption that you will have done all of your preparation exercises, and are de-cluttered, grounded, centered and ready to go!

If you have failed to prepare yourself properly, then it is only your own experience that you will be affecting, by preventing yourself from

getting the most from this wonderful Coddle-Popper experience.

Part 2 will be best if you use the CD of this book, and wear headphones to maximize the experience. But we have provided a written account for those more meticulous in their approach, who would like to take their time with their preparations.

The Coddle-Popper way is: 'Ready … **FIRE!** … Aim.'

As long as the Coddle-Poppers take care of the ducks, the rows will take care of themselves - so to speak.

Let the Universe unravel in all of its glory, because that's the only way the Universe works! Much like a Coddle-Popper, everything is done at the appropriate moment.

HOW TO SEE
THE FAERIES
THE COMPLETE CODDLE-POPPER GUIDE

PART 2

FINAL PREPARATIONS

Welcome back, and part two is the fun part; not that part one wasn't fun, but this is the difference between being given a new toy and now being allowed to play with it.

We left you at the end of part one, where we recommended that you put down the book, or pause the audio, in order that you take as much time as you needed, so as to de-clutter, ground, and center before we begin.

That being said, it is now our assumption that you have already done all of your preparation exercises, and that you are de-cluttered, grounded, centered and ready to 'rock and roll.'

We also recommend that you use the CD provided at the back of this book - wearing stereo headphones too, in order to enhance your experience.

WARNING: PLEASE DO NOT DO THIS WHILE OPERATING ANY KIND OF MACHINERY.

The journey to see the Coddle-Poppers is not a complicated process, and we will guide you at all times. The awesome Archangel Michael will

provide protection for us, so all you really need to do is follow the drums and your heart.

While you are meditating/journeying, we shall drum like this.

Drumming example

When it is time to finish and come back, you will notice first a falter in the rhythm, and then a change of tempo. We shall call you back and guide you into the present doing this.

Drumming example

That's a lot of stuff to take in in one squirt, so don't go worrying over it because we'll be doing a practice run in a moment, just to whet your whistle before we go off on our exciting journey to visit the Coddle-Poppers, for real!

SETTING YOUR INTENTION

Before we start our journey we need to set our intention, because if we don't know what we want ourselves, then how are the Faeries and Guardian Spirits supposed to know either?

So we're going to drum for about one minute, in order for you to concentrate on a question that you'd like to ask your Guardian Spirit, favourite Coddle-Popper or Faery. Maybe you'd like to have some healing instead, if that's what you might prefer.

Yes sir, it's not always about asking questions, sometimes it's good to mix it up a bit. You always get healing as part of your journey anyway, but focused healing makes you feel all warm and fuzzy just like a peach does in a sauna.

Whatever you choose, you must be very unambiguous with your question, or intention, in order to communicate it properly to your helping Spirit. Make sure that your intention or question is super-clear and unmistakable.

If your intention or question is wishy-washy or vague, then you can bet your bottom dollar that the wires will get crossed and your

answers back might be just as lack-lustre, or equally vague.

Now we're almost ready to start our journey. You can say your question out loud, or quietly to yourself in your mind and remember; always be courteous and polite to whomever you speak to, and don't be afraid to ask lots and lots more questions as you get each answer.

Coddle-Poppers and Faeries love questions, as they don't usually get humans for company very often. Well, not down in the 'Other World' anyway. And, if you don't ask the question, how can you get the answer?

PROTECTION

We call upon Archangel Michael to join us on our journey with the Coddle-Poppers to the 'Other World' and we respectfully ask for your mighty sword and shield for protection and allow us to lean upon your strength for courage. Thank you, thank you, thank you and so it is.

Keep your prayer to Archangel Michael simple, it doesn't need to be long or complicated. A few brief words straight from your heart, is far better than any elaborate string of memorized words that might sound good, but don't really have any feeling.

Now is a good time to mention that Archangel Michael is the 'Head-Honcho' when it comes to protection, and there's no one, nor no-thing in the Spirit World that dares mess with Archangel Michael. No sir!

It can now be said that we're in very safe hands, covered with bubble wrap with a front row seat for our adventure with the Coddle-Poppers to the 'Other World.'

If at any time you should wonder why your

Coddle-Popper, Faery or Guardian Spirit does not come close to you, please be aware that because of Archangel Michael's protection, this will mean that none of the Faery folk will be allowed to come close to you, **UNLESS** you invite them closer **AND** that their intentions are honourable.

The Faery folk do not wish to incur the intervention of Archangel Michael. No sir, not one little bit!

The onus will be on **YOU** to invite them to come closer, so that they might be allowed past Archangel Michael, knowing that they have your blessing.

Life will never be the same again once you expand the imagination to a new level of thinking. It will reveal a whole new dimension that exists right here in front of your very eyes, without you even realising. How exciting is that?

CONNECTION

It's now time to turn off your cell phone and make sure that you won't be disturbed for a half hour or so.

Put your headphones on and blindfold too, if you prefer your meditation in the dark.

Be sure to make yourself nice and comfy, sitting with your feet touching the ground and ready to give yourself the gift of some well-deserved **'me time.'**

Allow tree roots to grow from the soles of your feet, down into the ground. This will be your anchor and will keep you grounded, so let them grow deep and wide.

Feel a bright white light of energy shine from Source, down through your crown chakra above your head and allow it to immerse you from the top of your head, to the tips of your toes and out through your roots. Very much like you did in the centering exercise. It runs through every part of your being.

Okay, start to take some deep breaths, experiencing your breath moving through your entire body and mixing with the Source energy. You might like to place your hands on your heart,

or your belly, to feel the power of your breath.

Take a deep breath in …

Take a long cleansing breath out …

Again, a deep breath in … and let your mind quieten with a long breath out.

Repeat this a few times, at your own pace.

Are there any thoughts, feelings, sensations, or images that pop into your mind as you breathe? Notice the sounds around you.

Separate yourself from these thoughts and sounds and leave the clutter and chatter of everyday life behind for now.

We are going to follow the bright white light coming into our crown chakra upwards to its source, up through the clouds … all the way up into space … past all of the galaxies … into the next lot of galaxies that you didn't even know we had … through another bright white cloud, to the highest plain of Creator - where the energy and light is pure.

You are now before Creator, so open your heart and let your love and gratitude for all your blessing flow. The more appreciation you have, the more you get.

Now that you know how to visit Creator, you can come back to visit at any time - even if it's just for a hug.

'Hi Creator. Thank you for providing us with a means of safe passage to the 'Other World.' Please let my ego and personal intentions step aside for the greater good, and allow me to understand the wisdom and blessings of what I am shown. Thank you, thank you, thank you. And so it is.'

We shall follow the thread of pure light from Creator, going back down to your body, where you notice that it is waiting to enter your body through your heart chakra. Do not enter just yet.

This means that we now have peace of mind knowing that all of the energies we encounter on our meditation/journey are pure energies, as they come straight from Creator who loves us all unconditionally, and has only our best interests at heart.

Traditional ways of going down into the Lower World are through an opening into the earth, such as a cave, or a lake, river, or a waterfall. It could be a tree trunk, a volcano, or even a rabbit hole in the ground.

If it helps, use the doorway of the Coddle-Popper Sacred Stump that is pictured on the cover of this book. It matters not which way you choose to get into the earth; each of them are fine and dandy.

JOURNEY

So, let's begin our journey to the Lower World by thinking about a place in nature that you have been to, and can picture in your mind's eye.

Experience yourself being right there and notice if there's an entrance into the earth that you can use to travel down into the Lower World. Do not enter until I give the signal.

I will give you some time to look around and find an opening that you would like to try. For those having difficulties, I shall describe what I see as I journey, and you may follow along doing the same in your own mind's eye.

I am picturing a mossy tree stump in the woods, with what looks like a Faery-style Edwardian period wooden door.

The tree stump is cleverly situated behind a second tree stump, which keeps it hidden safely out of sight from anyone with an untrained eye.

It is a beautiful place; quiet, moist, and the rays of the sun can still reach it. This is the portal that we shall use. It can only be located and entered into from the heart chakra.

I see my heart chakra as being a shaman's doorway, with lots of leaves around the edges.

When I am ready, my heart chakra opens and a bright light shines from my chest, to fuse with the bright white light from Creator, to let him in, and this is my signal to enter my body and begin my journey.

I am the size of a Coddle-Popper and I am now able to see the world through their eyes.

I can see my mossy tree stump portal and I enter through the bright light shining through the cracks of the faery door. The light is also a bright white. I open the door and I see an elevator in front of me.

For those of you with your own special place, imagine that you are opening into the earth, experience yourself entering into the opening and you will find yourself in a transition that might appear as a tunnel, or portal of some kind, that leads you into the Lower World.

Mine is an elevator.

There is a button inside that says 'Other World.'

Press it.

For those who prefer to take the stairs, follow

the tunnel down or take the elevator while saying to yourself:

'I wish to meet my ... (insert Coddle-Popper, Faery or Guardian Spirit) **... in the Lower World.'**

As you walk down your tunnel or transition, feel your feet and the ground beneath you. Notice how it feels. Is it soft, hard, bumpy or smooth? If you're in the elevator, feel the vibrations as you drop deeper into the earth.

Are you ready? I'm going to open the doors now and remember that all is safe. It's going to be fun.

Step forward into the light and emerge into the Lower World.

Feel the air on your skin. Is the air cool, warm, wet or dry? Breathe in all the fragrances.

What is the sky like? Are there clouds or is it sunny?

You are in a place of great beauty and peace.

Feel the earth beneath you; notice whether the ground you are standing on is hard or soft, moist or dry. Are you standing on leaves? Is

it grass or sand? Maybe it's another quality of the Earth.

We shall walk along the riverbank towards the sleepy little Coddle-Popper village of Buttercup Meadow in the Wood.

Notice the heron standing on one leg fishing at the water's edge.

The sound of the shallow river is soothing. Hold out your hand and brush your palms along the tops of the rushes. Feel the coarseness and resistance.

In the distance you can just about hear the celebrations going on at Buttercup Meadow in the Wood. If you remembered to bring your chocolate, now would be a great time to dig it out of your pocket. Get ready ...

The Coddle-Poppers and Faeries are here to greet us. They are lined up along the side of the pathway, waving most eagerly.

They've agreed not to make a sound, or come over to you, in order not to alarm those of us here for the first time.

For the more seasoned meditation/journeyers, perhaps you might like to go over to the

Coddle-Poppers, strike up a conversation and share out your chocolate.

Look at their little faces light up. How special and magical is that? I'll bet you never imagined that giving could be so much fun.

Notice too, that even though you are the one doing the giving, you are receiving so much more in return.

Isn't it a magical and fantastic feeling?

The Coddle-Poppers and Fairies will not touch you, unless you give them permission to.

It is a very special occasion for Coddle-Poppers having a human come to visit, so take a while to soak in the joy and magical energy.

Notice your surroundings; suck in the excitement of all the Coddle-Poppers. What emotions do you feel at being honoured in such great esteem?

We shall hang on here just for a short while to give you time to say hello to the Coddle-Poppers, because they have been so excited about meeting us and they especially want to say hello to you.

They've waited such a long time and it is a real privilege for them.

A short while later ...

We're going to move on now. The Coddle-Poppers have agreed to stay here and look after the Coddle-berry wine, and it is the Fairies who are going to be our guides.

We shall continue along the path of the river-bank. Notice the colours, the different plants and animal life, and experience the glorious sounds of nature.

On the other side of the river is a meandering path leading deeper into the woods.

What you hear in the distance are the singing trees. We are going to walk through them later, whilst they sing.

To cross the shallow river and get to the singing trees, there are three stepping-stones.

The brook is not deep and you can see the stones on the bottom of the shallow pools.

You step onto the first stone and notice a small fish dart between you and the second stepping stone. The beauty of his scales shimmering in the sun, illuminates your face.

You step onto the second stone and crouch down to look at your reflection in the clear pool.

Notice how happy you look, how being in nature makes you feel better, how the energy of the water makes you relaxed.

Put your non-dominant hand into the water and let the brook carry away your troubles. Feel the coolness on your fingers and watch as you see the days niggles wash away. Take a long breath out. Life is good!

You stand back up and step onto the last stone and notice that the music at the Coddle-Popper village of Buttercup Meadow in the Wood, has stopped and that the singing from the trees is calling you.

The last hop to the other side of the brook is a gentle step and you step safely over.

You keep walking along the path until you get to the singing trees.

Hold your hand out and touch the trunk of one of the singing trees. Feel its creases; notice the different smells in the air, the sun shining through the canopy of leaves onto your face.

The trees are singing a sound that helps them

expand their awareness and enjoyment of life.

How does the vibration of their singing make you feel?

Feel the Om cleansing your aura.

We shall carry on walking again, but slowly so that we can soak in the wonderful, therapeutic energy that's being created by the singing trees.

On the other side of the singing trees, you notice a clearing up ahead and head towards it. As you get closer you notice a rock, big enough for two people to sit on. You head towards it and sit down on it. It feels warm from being in the sun. The gentle warm breeze feels wonderful on your face, as you soak in the sun's rays.

Look around you; listen for, or feel if there is a Coddle-Popper, Faery or Guardian Spirit waiting to greet you.

Become aware of a loving, helping Spirit.

If it does not look like a Coddle-Popper or Faery, ask the helping Spirit,

'Are you my Guardian Spirit?'

The Spirit might answer you telepathically, or it might lead you somewhere, or show you some-

thing that indicates the Spirit is there to help you.

You may have a gut feeling in your body that gives you the sense that the Spirit is there for you.

Now ask your Coddle-Popper, Faery or Guardian Spirit why it has come into your life. Ask:

'What do you have to teach me?'

We shall now drum in silence for a few minutes while your Coddle-Popper, Faery or Guardian Spirit shares its role in your life.

Remember to state your question, intention or request for healing to your helping Spirit and just experience what happens next.

Use all of your senses. Look, listen, hear, feel and smell. There are many ways your helping Spirit will reveal answers to you and provide healing.

Or if you don't feel comfortable calling them closer, just use this time to simply enjoy spending some quality time with your helping Spirit friend and just **BE** together.

A short while later ...

It is now time to start saying your goodbyes.

Before leaving, ask your Coddle-Popper, Faery or Guardian Spirit:

'What strength do you hold?'

Ask your Coddle-Popper, Faery or Guardian Spirit to touch your hands and pass this gift on to you. I will drum briefly while you receive the strength from your helping Spirit.

A short while later ...

It's now time to come back. Notice the change in drum tempo as it's time to leave.

THE RECALL

Thank your helping Spirit for the help and love you have received.

Let your helping Spirit know that it is time for you to return home to the Middle World and say goodbye for now.

We shall go back the same way that we came taking with you all you have gained from this experience.

Begin to journey back, knowing that this experience will create positive benefits in your daily life, and when you get back, you will be able to remember your experience and record it in your journal.

Begin to journey back, following the drum beat, turn around and begin to leave. Leave this beautiful healing place, and retrace your steps back through the singing trees … over the three stepping stones of the brook … through the sleepy Coddle-Popper village of Buttercup Meadow in the Wood … back along the riverbank path to the elevator.

Step in to the elevator and wave goodbye to the Coddle-Poppers as the door closes. Notice how the Coddle-berry wine makes their cheeks

go rosy and how much it makes their eyes sparkle.

Press the elevator button that says **'Home'** and the elevator will take you back to the Faery door ... step out of the elevator and you're back outside the Coddle-Popper Sacred Stump. Go back through your heart chakra, and stay in the bright light up to Creator.

'That was awesome. Thank you, thank you, thank you Creator. Love you.'

Back through the clouds ... through the galaxy that you didn't know about ... through the galaxy that you did ... down through the clouds ... and in through your crown chakra and you are back into your body again.

'Thank you, thank you, thank you Archangel Michael for your company and protection.'

When you are ready, and it feels right, take a few deep, grounding breaths, wiggle your toes and fingers, place your hands on your heart and connect with your heartbeat.

Bring your awareness to your eyes, and as you open them, slowly come back into the room.

Feel your body. Take some time in silence to

review the information you received from your Coddle-Popper, Faery or Guardian Spirit.

Notice if you are feeling any different because of the healing you received.

Feel yourself fully back in your body, completely grounded and connected. Welcome home.

When you are ready, and in your own time, remove anything that you have had over your eyes.

Say thank you for your life and all the wonderful people and things in it.

Was that exciting or what?

You might now wish to take some notes of your experience while it is still fresh for you.

The most wonderful thing about this experience is that you can repeat this journey, time and time again, in order to meet your helping Spirit.

WINK

This is Wink. Wink is our 'go to' guy and he's in charge of all the administration duties here at Faery Wood. We rely on him heavily as our point of contact with all matters to do with faery. He takes great pride in his work and is meticulous in his attention to detail. For anything to do with Faery Wood or Healing Owl … **wink@faerys.ca**

WANT TO LEARN MORE ABOUT THE CODDLE-POPPERS?

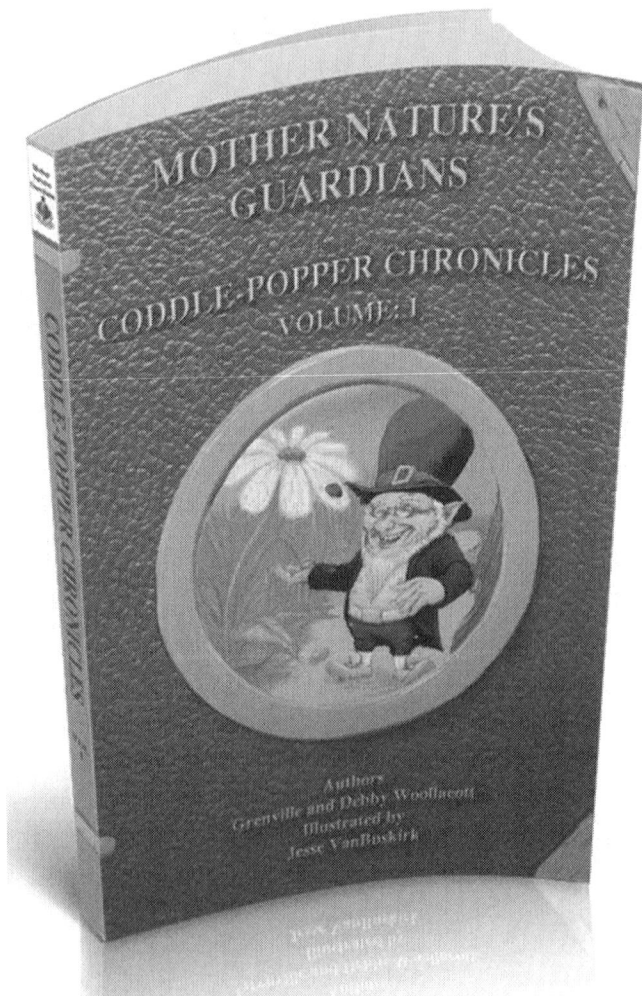

MOTHER NATURE'S GUARDIANS

CODDLE-POPPER CHRONICLES

VOLUME: 1

Authors
Grenville and Debby Woollacott
Illustrated by
Jesse VanBuskirk

SPECIAL THANKS

When a book has been made with so much love poured into it, that love needed to have come from somewhere. We happen to feel exceptionally fortunate to have been blessed with so many wonderful people in our lives.

We can't name them all because that would take another whole book in order to list just half of them, but here are just a few of the most extraordinary of the extraordinary people in our lives, and they're listed in no particular order. We love you all and thank you.

My best friend Gerald Bourque, who has a heart the size of a mountain; Nichole Jacobson for all that she has done for Debby; Alan Edwards, Dale McBride and Drew Kennickell, our 'go to' guys, where nothing is too much trouble; & Gracie-Mae, who proved that miracles really do happen!

Additional thank yous to Jenny Jobbins, Patricia Garrod, Connie Burtt, Joan Harty, and especially Dad, Nanny & Grandad, who made this whole dream possible.

Let's also not forget the real heroes and brains of this outfit ... Spirit, the Coddle-Poppers and all the Faery folk. We're just the eye candy.

The
Coddle-Popper
Storybook I

Grenville & Debby
Woollacott

Wood

The
Fairy Stone
Storybook II

Grenville & Debby
Woollacott

Faery Wood

The
TREE OF WISHES
Storybook III

Grenville & Debby
Woollacott

Faery Wood

Storybook IV
Thomas 'Tipsy' Tippleman

Grenville & Debby
Woollacott

Faery Wood

OTHER BOOKS IN THE SERIES

'Mother Nature's Guardians'
Coddle-Popper Chronicles Vol: I

'How to see the Faeries'
The Complete Coddle-Popper Guide

COMING SOON

MINI SERIES STORYBOOKS

Storybook 1: **'The Coddle-Popper'**
Audio only

Storybook 2: **'The Fairy Stone'**
Audio only

Storybook 3: **'The Tree of Wishes'**
Audio only

Storybook 4: **'Thomas 'Tipsy' Tippleman'**
Audio only

www.**FaeryWood**.com

www.**ThunderPalms**.com

www.facebook.com/thelandofthelittlepeople

JOURNAL NOTES

JOURNAL NOTES

JOURNAL NOTES

JOURNAL NOTES

JOURNAL NOTES

Made in the USA
San Bernardino, CA
06 June 2016